**Poetry by Houston A. Baker, Jr.**

*No Matter Where You Travel, You Still Be Black*
*Spirit Run*
*Blues Journeys Home*

# Blues Journeys Home

### New and Selected Poems

by

## Houston A. Baker, Jr.

### Illustrated by Jeff Donaldson

**LOTUS PRESS**
Detroit
1985

Copyright 1985 by Houston A. Baker, Jr.

First Edition
All rights reserved

International Standard Book Number 0-916418-61-8
Library of Congress Catalog Card Number 85-80142

PS
3552
.A427
B5
1985

Lotus Press, Inc.
Post Office Box 21607
Detroit, Michigan 48221

*In Memory of My Father,
Houston A. Baker, Sr.*

## Acknowledgments

The author wishes to thank James Olney for including a number of poems that appear in the present volume in a recent issue of **The Southern Review.** He is grateful as well for Naomi Long Madgett's permission to reprint poems that appeared in earlier volumes of his work published by Lotus Press. And he feels enormous gratitude for a grant from the Research Foundation of the University of Pennsylvania which helped to finance the present volume and made possible the brilliant illustrations by Jeff Donaldson.

## Contents

### I. Kin

This Is Not a Poem ... 11
City of My Youth ... 12
Return to My Parents' Home ... 13
My Mother's Mother's House ... 14
Carolina, Coltrane, and Love ... 15
Socializing Roots ... 16
Sasquatch in the South ... 17

### II. Guardians

The Patriarch ... 21
Toward Guinea ... 22
Of Walter White's Father in the Rain ... 23
Edinburgh, 1967-68 ... 24
For Hosea Hudson ... 25
Brother Zeke ... 27
A Poem for Gus Cannon ... 28
A Redeeming Word ... 29
The Poet's Funeral in Winter ... 30

## III. Earth and Ancestors

<u>Sr:</u>
Sd   For an African Chronicle ............................. 32

Jordan ................................................... 33

Exchange on a Southern Road ........................... 35

Four Acres: Sans Mule ................................. 36

Southern Noon ......................................... 37

Winter's Inclemencies ................................. 38

Winter Grace .......................................... 39

Found Woman ........................................... 40

Southern City, Across the Track ....................... 41

Clean Trucks and Sunday Clothes ....................... 42

Memory of Kin ......................................... 43

Double South Spring ................................... 44

In the Break .......................................... 45

In Town: Saturday ..................................... 47

Southern Ending ....................................... 48

## IV. Downhome Blues

Middle Passage Blues .................................. 50

Blues Beneath the Skin ................................ 51

Train Whistle in Rain ................................. 52

Southern Sunrise ...................................... 53

Tobacco Warehouse Blues ............................... 54

Another Man ........................................... 55

A Bible Lesson ........................................ 56

Flying Home ........................................... 57

Prodigal .............................................. 59

# I
# Kin

## This Is Not a Poem

This is not a poem, nor
Aesthetic experience.
This is the story of my grandmother's
Hands chapped from white folks' wash,
An account of her back spasmed
From scrubbing floors.
This is not a poem, nor
Icey "art emotion."
This is a narrative of my father's father
Scraping pennies from a rocky economy.
Depression devouring everything in sight.
This is no poem, nor
Subtle tingle down your spine while shaving:
This is a tale of my mother
Rebuked for calling a black man "gentleman":

("Lizzie, tell your daughter, *niggers* are not gentlemen!")

This is no poem, nor
Am I blessed to be impersonal.
I will make no attempt to distance you.
Had you been there while I was growing up, or
Even in the thin/worn time of their decline,
I would have introduced you.
Allowed you to share the fine goodness of ancestral
Caring.

## City of My Youth

A seed-time of quick violence
And hours resonant with despair,
Growing in this southern town
Was against the law,
Each green shoot lopped off. . .

There was no sunshine six days a week;
On Sunday it beamed for ecstatic religion, and
Settled at dusk to a blood-red and sinful sky.

Finding my way through texts on family shelves,
I talked of **Candide** and Copernicus
To the stunned horror of others,
Became prey to charges of literacy
As hooked knives of the South swung low
To carry me home:
Black sufferers demanded my head
(on a platter)
And white women hinted worse.

Through this spawning time I read on, praying
For a moment to confide its truth,
In later hours ringing with despair,
To engage the burden of literacy (thank God!)
In the open air.

**Return to My Parents' Home, Christmas, 1979**

The first hour is embrace
and careful silence, avoiding
vulnerabilities
and obvious change
you reach for the boy
you left behind,

sense his fear
when stepping from the last stair
into the third-floor night,
a room of charm and fetish
secure against the monsters of his day,
notorious boogies
and Southern Whites. . . his head falling toward
the pillow, a prayer, a sensual sleep. . .

Shadows in the jolly corner
recall the wonder of those days,
as you search the vesper of your parents' eyes
and find once more the strength
of their undiminished love.

Your son looks on, awaits his turn, as
the season begins again.

**My Mother's Mother's House**

Arriving at midnight,
The pitch street makes no sound,
Squat houses are lightless,
A patchwork of stars hangs low.
My mother gently taps and calls: "Mother."
A sleepy sound, muffled inside, responds,
Takes form at the opened door as my "cousin" Raymond
(Boy adopted when his Mother "went wild.")
"Well, well, y'all managed to get here after all."
My Grandmother pushes through a curtain between rooms,
And hugs us all.
The voices overlap in rushes of affection.
The stove's final embers pop.
Tomorrow, we shall tolerate an old radio's crackling,
Listen in harmony to entertainment from afar.
Already, I taste bittersweet cobbler,
Already know, with boy's sleepy intuition,
That good times are with ancestors;
Their memories are blues voices
Moving through an infinity of years.

## Carolina, Coltrane, and Love

Grey, autumn squirrel scoots
Across a distant branch,
Sunlight slashes trees,
Revealing textures in Saturday light
Rare as earth itself.

*(In my livingroom John Coltrane plays Naima.)*

The old gold and stubborn green of Carolina are
Flavored by a neighbor's smoke.

*(There is a shaman chanting — torturous — older than earth.)*

As my son awakens with a boisterous yawn.

*(A horn invoking chaos, creating comfort — ordering African spirit.)*

Today we will complete his African project.
Working together at rituals ancient as the seasons old.

*(Chordal progressions blast barriers! Shaman
gives birth to the world.)*

The squirrel is at our deck.
Dry leaves and sheets of sound,
We discuss forests and rivers
Older than the signs of man.

*(On my disc, Naima gives way to Om, a single hand — clapping)*

Charlotte awakens, stretches toward the sun:

**She is motion and energy, embodiment of spirits called.
The ending is Black.
The ending is Love.
The ending of African genius is (always) love.**

## Socializing: Roots: Or When My Wife Surprised the Dinner Party with Talk of Her Youth

I see you in North Carolina dawns,
Your knees rattling against the morning chill,
Yellow pump water in six-years hands.
Your city-born Mom has launched you South with toothpaste,
Toilet tissue — warning off dirt, and the country.
You return from the field with foaming mouth,
Butt of rural jokes, with flattened toilet rolls in
Your possession — no Sears Catalogue for your tender bottom.
Undaunted, you meet the sun with your own etchings in dust,
Shell dried corn for your Grandfather's **biddies**.
Tough birds all. . .
Your words return southern accents,
Sources of your excellence hidden
Until now.

## Sasquatch in the South

Under a gray sky in Sunday's South
A Black Boy beckons
Calling the man to enter Carolina woods.

This Sabbath search began in fantasy:
A book on Big Foot, a buddy willing to play,
And on this day,
Armed with instamatic, flash cubes at the ready, he
Has entranced a patriarch's desire
For heathen pioneer, rugged redskin,
Catalytic cowboy days ready to act — sport longpast.

A soggy path leads school boys on weekdays.
Deserted now, left to chipmunks and inquisitive
Squirrels busy with fall.

They descend, picking choicest stones for foundation.
Building hope along the way:
"You're too slow, Dad!"
Hurled back as he begins to run, reaching the
Streamed bottom in breathless flight.

The man finds the spot, leaps stones and lands.

"This way!"

They find the key to this endeavor:
A moist depression in earth that could be
Faulkner's bear, or,
Some raucous hoarde of patterrollers in the night.

"Doesn't it look like Big Foot's print?"

He hesitates,
Nods assent to boy's relief.
A simple credulity registered
In the man's finger pointing,
The flash cube's sudden flare —
A caption leaps to mind:

"September 20, 1982 — Today we found evidence of the Beast."

*Beast/mystery of downhome soil,*
*The specific lineaments*
*Of an imagined history,*
*Not without terror of lynching trees and gross politicians,*
*For whom footprints in Nigger sand were no joke...*
*Beast/mystery does not hold him long.*

He returns to the gray present, prays
His son will always recall,
How fierce ancestral love
Brought them out alive.

# II
## Guardians

**The Patriach**
for Sterling Brown

Tobacco, blackened fragments
Left behind
Your slow-footed departure.
Spinner of the old tales,
Corn-cob carrier of blues:

*Went to the depot, looked at de bo'de,*
*Lawd, went to de depot, looked at de bo'de,*
*Say it's good times here, it's better up de road.*

A tough switch engine
Moving lots of tons,
Mr. Brown puffin'
A fuel noways done!

## Toward Guinea: For Larry Neal, 1937-1981

I remember your strut.
Disguised as Garvey's ghost,
You entered the room.
Your plumed stride and narrow eyes
Matched the peacock's radiant glory.
You gave the shout of Shine,
Bellowed like James Brown,
Swam miraculously against white currents.
And now you have left. . .

Tomorrow's dawn will find you moving toward Guinea:
Jamming again on African ground,
A bright reunion
Of ancestral sound.

## Of Walter White's Father in the Rain

Horrified when they realized their
patient's race, the medical staff
promptly ceased its labors and sent
Walter White's father bumping across the
street in driving rain to the dilapidated
building reserved for Afro-Americans.

(from *When Harlem Was In Vogue*)

Denied,
Like Bessie,
Bleeding in southern rain,
You felt your body jolted
Above gurney wheels,
Water driving into your
Pain-filled eyes.
Your bones shattered by
The physician's speeding car
Cried for mercy,
Some balm to still the agony,
And hazily you recall
First moments in the
White wards:
Soft faces of concern
And antiseptic efficiency;
Monitors' quiet beeping;
Now, like Bessie on back roads dying,
You are discovered a son of Ham,
A son-in-law's dark inquiry set the staff humming:

"God-damned **Nigger**. . . My God!"

You feel your crushed body jolted,
Rolling through rain to a colored hospital's
Crumbling wards of rats and decay.
You will pass before day is done.

Evening etches your sons' future,
With Southern rain drops in acid detail,
Rehearses a blues melody of the Empress dying.
Passing in the rain, separate,
And forever unequalled.

### Edinburgh, 1967-68

There was the surprise of her sadness,
Standing in the fog light's prismatic glow
She wept for home.

But like the lost sound,
Salt on icy pavements long ago,
Rain over the morning window brought bells,
The flash of steeples in gray air,
And an unctious parson saluted us.

We moved by the Firth at night,
Walking its still, moist bed
And heard the foghorn's beat from distant Fife.
The last rumble and far away flame of American cities
Became less real than yesterday's post.

And when the park by the sea was empty,
Its roundabout beginning to rust,
We huddled against the wind, labored
With omnibuses uphill, and heard the blue
goodbyes of schoolboys.
Our salvation was an aged lady talking of her Ken

("The fighter, you know?")
And flannel sheets.

April brought the news: THE KING IS DEAD? THE KING
HAS BEEN KILLED IN MEMPHIS! THE KING IS DEAD.

That night we wept in a farm cottage,
Cold as Dante's heads just above water — Startled.
At daybreak we passed daffodils to surprised provincials,
Knowing that spring — a return in confusion —
Was to come.

**For Hosea Hudson, Black Communist Worker, at 79**

The pungent odor of vapor rub and
Too many hours without sun
Or the season's quick wind
Through broken screens,
The compact chairs bursting their limits,
Stuffing exposed to
Bright, dim, gray ancestors across the walls,
The browning of a bare bulb on the table
Laden with *Political Affairs* —
Refrigerator clicks, hums low in a farther room,
As counterpoint, as low voice without judgment,
In the tape recorder's whirring:

"Not everyone can be in the Party.
The Party don't mind yo' havin' a friend.
But they don't want you hopping from limb
to limb like no bantam rooster. . ."

The cassettes change.
Scene unfolds in mute significance.
Eyes along the wall, under table glass,
On a mantle's ledge
Become family:

"That's my mother."
(She is faint, unripe candidate
for his dark voice.)
"And the cousin I told you 'bout, her daughter,
an aunt — my mother's sister."

He is drawn back by the sharp fight of dogs:

"Every afternoon, every afternoon — but that weren't
my point. You see there ain't no such thing as
'higher-ups'. What you got is Democratic Centralism.
The majority decide and then all the bickering got
to stop."

Dogs crackle through the room,
Releasing violent eyes along the wall.

Avoiding the frame of his dead wife in coffin,
I inquire about the overalled black man and
Solemn black companion.

"Yes, sho, that's Sarg' Carfield,
his brother-in-law,
down in Baton Rouge.
Befo' he lost his strength."
The light dims and resumes:
"I'm old now, but I still believes."

## Brother Zeke
for Ezekiel Mphahlele

Last year we ate duck *à l'orange*
and drank a fine *claret*
your gracious laughter bubbling 'round
the table, reminding us that we had never known
the darkness rolling — the austere loneliness —
inside:
*"Ah, mon frère, mon frère, comme tu es très gentil!"*
from you above ground.

And we did not know, Ezekiel,
the strong voices calling,
the drumvoices beating,
the many voices summoning you from us;
South Africa was distant, cruel, and very hard
to comprehend.

Now we think of your seat in the candle's vague shadow,
Evening of the bantustan closing fast,
(Ah, brother Zeke, you are so gentle!)

We are calling you this day,
We are summoning your strong laughter,
We are lonely, Ezekiel, and afraid.

Children of the Western storm, brother Zeke,
We seek your voice
To lead us home.

## A Poem for Gus Cannon

A raccoon skin, scraped thin
For resonance,
A guitar neck and old bread pan
Made you a stomper,
Medicine show traveller,
Jug band man for southern barbecues
And rollicking barrelhouses.

Your long frame became
An instrument of peer delight:
Men in plantation fields held you in awe.
Brown girls with big eyes
Hummed at your strumming.
And around Memphis everyone took pride
In your store-bought banjo and sharp-creased pants:

"Gus Cannon," you would say,
"Gus Cannon's Jug Stompers."
"Here to let you know what country blues is all about!"

And then you made them, Gus,
*"Drop down, Mama,/Sweet as the showers of rain."*

**A Redeeming Word: For Hoyt W. Fuller, 1923-1981**

Preacher said you were like
The word, African man of new beginning,
Unflowerlike essence of things,
All the embalming clay of Georgia
Can not erase the history you made:
African words for a first world,
Powerful words for a New World
You led us all to see.

### The Poet's Funeral in Winter

The morning ice was unbeatable,
Sliding across lanes and down avenues,
We were prepared for sorrow.
A dawn express to the metropole,
Where you would be interred,

Surprised by death, you thought your last pain a rehearsal.

At the holy door strings sound,
Haunting signifiers by ladies in black,
Who knew your life (intimately).
They are veiled sibyls,
Playing out the darkness still to come.
My trip to the men's room carries me past your picture's
Stare, down stairs smelling of cheap furniture polish,
And opens into the Church's day room.
Ragamuffin people everywhere, old bloods, last night's
Raunchy winos, big-butted black women, and smells
of greasy sustenance — coffee brewing.
They do not know you are dead.
In this instance, I know the meaning
Of your living.

# III
# Earth Ancestors

**Sr\***
---
**Sd:   for an African Chronicle**

Here, below the line,
Is our ancestral yard,
Replete with codicils and broken-necked guitars;
Pine-needle bed of history.

Above the bar,
An endless play of signifiers,
Harmonica bridges,
Gut-bucket connectives that
Span black time,
All blue.

---

\* A Standard designation in semiotics (the science of signs) for signifier (sr) or word and signified (sd) or meaning.

## Jordan

Our sharp cry
Engaged the circling grove:
*Lawd, I washed my head in the mid-night dew!*
(Our end was distant.)
*The morning stars a witness, too.*

We sang a road, a powerful long ladder through southern air
to heaven,
A lonesome journey beyond fields where human life
*Oh, de debbil is a liar and a conjurer, too*
Was held in fee.
*An 'ef you don't mind he'll conjure you!*

As mourners we sought
The river's rich growth.
Enduring and resourceful, we sang:
*I'm sometimes up and sometimes down,*
In our voice we felt
*But still my soul is Canaan bound!*
A free shore rising.

**Exchange on a Southern Road**

He is monumental presence
Against southern pine
And slashes of dogwood-red in autumn.
His limp is tell-tale sign
Of hard days behind the mule.

Now, weathered and philosophic,
He salutes the car with northern plates,
Whose driver recalls scraps of tobacco in a leather chair,
The smell of smoke in sunshine and afterchurch certainty of love,
A "smoketown" dignity given him to live. . .

A blues spark along high voltage lines,
Connects a race of men.

### Four Acres: Sans Mule

The coca-cola sign is vintage '30s,
Era of lean crops and sallow crackers,
Time of national malaise and slim pickin',
His mother escaped to Big Easy with a travellin' man.
The fields around are ageless.
Poverty has not altered their face since the War.
Returning home mercifully alive,
He resumed traces of his birth.
Began a new dawn where yesteryears left off,
Working.

### Southern Noon

Smoke-blackened wood holds memories
Of lean days and children underfoot.
John slapping leather on a mule's reluctant butt,
Frosted breath of muscled man and beast
Are visible when she pauses;
A cold window on survival, as his
Plow jerks to slow furrow.
Shifting the baby to her good arm,
She ladles yesterday's soup for supper.
He will bounce the child once before washing,
Finish a hasty meal.
He stores defiance for sunset:
A single bold holler at the very close of day.

**Winter's Inclemencies**

Winter's deserted morning road,
Rain slanting furiously down,
The man leans into a subtle curve
Of browned foliage and sharp pines.
His mind retreats to a voodoo woman of youth,
Summer trips by these same trees,
And jaunty words for firefly nights:
"Some day, Johnson, that **FOLLOW-ME-HOME-DUST**
go'ne have its way!"
Mounded laughter as her twirled skirts
Brushed the porch's rails,
Then stroll through cotton-dark to home. . .

Thunder blossoms,
He remembers winter emptinesses,
Can not conjure her again
This Carolina dawn.

**Winter Grace**

The smell of dung in chill air,
Vast openness of fields now bare,
A fine mist falling since midnight
Has frosted a cabin roof.

Laborers uniformly clad build a fire.
Whose smoke reminds her of curing days of youth,
A sufficiency quite disappeared.

Wrapping wool about still shapely shoulders,
She takes coffee to the silent men,
Who are suddenly ominous,
Shadows of a dancing past.

Quietly, they thank her for this grace.
Blessed for brutal labor,
Another day commences,
On the road.

**Found Woman**

The yard is refulgent,
Overstuffed with wildflowers,
Lost pickup pieces,
Erotic grasses reddening in autumn.
The porch is spare, where
A swing holds her brown body as potential,
Motion.

(Children call from the creek.)

A man leans (ears keen) from a car.
He is struck by her still, born, beauty.
Discovers time's exactions manifold.
Scarifications bountiful as wildflowers.
Only a harmonica's blue subtleties (he regrets)
Are equal to such wailing,
Presence.

## Southern City, Across the Track

He tells a southern story
To disinterested whites,
Whose mirror gives back
Only skin-deep insight, or sin.
Says:
"We crossed modern tracks
Beside the Red Cross barracks,
And cityscapes decay,
Displayed propane tanks on rotting legs,
Yards that were archives of desperate days.
The smoke was sluggishly rising,
Wrapping like vines around
The once-stylish **Tire Company.**
We imagined yesterday's scene of sporty cars, dapper men in straw brims
Sporting their stuff for handy mechanics.
Startled, we found her mother's street.
She rocks in a roomful of memory.
Fearful of the blood-sport beyond her door, where
Black boys with shaved heads are out-of-work,
Shoot up in the southern night,
By the **Tire Company.**
Murder most relentless in their heart.
We could not persuade her away,
She saying:
'This been my home forever,
Ain't no use to leave it now.'
And that was all; a few embarrassed bills we left.
Made our escape to tenderer geographies,
Quite undone."

Whites nod, uncomprehending.
Their own mothers (like their souls) are stored
In antiseptic vaults,
On the Right side of the track.

## Clean Trucks and Sunday Clothes

Furrowed cumulus mark afternoon's end,
As he burnishes last chrome.
The pickup's wonder is its power to corner Carolina curves,
Frightening coons at dawn,
Roaring by autumnal squirrels,
And whizzing rain glazed roads, lights blazing.
He touches a shimmering antenna,
And dreams tomorrow's sunrise.
A Sunday suit severely creased awaits his adornment.

Years past Vietnam,
He relishes these pleasures:
Sunday suits and pickups shining clean.
A dark and simple settling of the land.

**Memory of Kin**

Violence of the storm's attending
Gives trees a graceful sway,
Yet, stared at long enough
The whole wood and world begin to move,
Summoning memories of ancestral departure,
Recalls a boy's self viewing the storm's work,
Never left the window 'til weepin' folks returned.
"Nanny's gone," was all his dad could muster.
His mother, buffeted like trees,
Moved unbelieving in the doorway's arch.
At night, restless branches kept him awake,
Whispered voices of
A wood and world now changed,
Forever.

## Double South Spring

Oak tassles descend
Covering earth with green goofer dust;
Pollen-bearing bees divebomb the shadow's silence,
And these are the makings of Faulknerian voices,
Caldwellian harmonies and Walker Percy gentles;
Beside spring roads wisteria weeps its scent
And masters and their descendants are a ghostly
Chorus, a white May dream.

Down back roads,
In cinder hovels, unweeded plots of paint-peeling shanties,
Nothing is happening.
No new-season resonance moves a progeny of harrowing rows.
Black folk survive by sound alone,
Are in-mates of a single season,
A timeless ritual of
Black and battered guitars.

**In the Break**

William and Minnie
(known as Hotstuff and Dot),
Blues lovers at Doc's,
Lock in moist embrace,
Rehearse ancient rhythms:
The syncopation of lost crops,
Offbeat of muddy waters rising,
The percussion of survival years, useless.
They hold fast 'til the last
Musician's rest;
Push back, in cool, wet blackness.
This moment's smile will not soften winter fields,
But suits the break, j'es fine.

**In Town: Saturday**

Baring trees surround the town green.
Their wind-sheared slendering
Deposits old gold, rich copper, as
Autumn bakes farmers, knotted at corners.
Children, whose distance from southern earth is determinant,
Loiter in arcades.
Soon, their wasted gold, handsome bronze,
Will cover new ground.
Leaving wind-sheared stalks
To guard ancestral soil.

## Southern Ending

No one was prepared for the breakdown of Big John,
225-lbs.-man, muscled to the "T."
Raucous baller of jacks and sometimes tenant farmer,
Strong engine wiper from Mississippi,
And singer on Jacksonville streets.
Could heist a pickup with handy ease.

No one was prepared to see his form laid low,
Stretched on shabby bed in a smokey room,
Rain slanting down the dirty glass and
Last family assembled in winter's fading light.

No one was prepared for his breakdown
Of facts before passing,
Capturing blind-riding days and streamboat nights:
"Son" (wheezed softly)
"Don't never 'low yo'self to confuse a quiet man with dumb."
Then trailing into an inaudible hum.

He was a blues moment at close of day,
A right fit rhythm,
For which
No one was prepared.

# IV
# Downhome Blues

## Middle Passage Blues

Out in mid-ocean, brother
Away from a familiar shore,
Out in mid-ocean, brother,
Far from a familiar shore,
Feel the chains in my soul, brother,
Can't hear drums no more.

Train whistle welcome me,
To this New World,
Train whistle welcome me,
To this New World,
Sliding on the blinds, Babe,
To a fine Black girl.

Far from the ocean, brother,
Caught on the blinds,
Train whistle make me whole, Babe,
Black girl ease my mind!

## Blues Beneath the Skin

Winter makes sedge brittle and brown,
Barren trees are signs of loss;
Plows can't move this rocky ground,
Locked in stone and early-morning's frost.
We take refuge in warm memories of kin,
Survive cold discouragement,
With blues beneath our skin:
Like black, ancestral kin,
We manage cold disaster,
With blues beneath our skin.

## Train Whistle in Rain

The train whistle in rain
Rolls through muted air
Across neighboring hills
And spreads its lonesome moisture
Through cabin insides.
Gray morning rituals blessed by
This far-off sign of hope,
This evidence of motion's relentless possibility,
Unseen,
Salvation,
Like glory locomotives,
Soon to come.

**Southern Sunrise**

Moving in morning mist,
Fall birds speak of snow and dogwoods shadowed by dark,
The big man draws a trucking company cap against the chill,
Adjusts overalls a size too small, and smiles.
He has not released this land to new highways, condominiums,
Remembers his grandfather's wit beneath the elm felled last year.
Hears a running brook mixed with childhood games, and gazes
Farther than the next hill to re-think adventures far from home.

*(O, stern labor and rollicking shake of a levee camp's learning!)*

As morning dew creeps through battered shoes,
He laughs in the sun's rising face,
Raises kin
With a blues shout
At the very break of day.

## Tobacco Warehouse Blues

The bluesman in pungent mood,
Has a parallax of shining rails in mind,
When he shouts of riding the blinds,
In the warehouse's second story,
One tale of fields/the other of this moment's song,
Escape from gang labor and long ride beneath the whale's belly,
A prophetic moment as plants took life,
And he and his guitar "up" from Georgie,
Made black men's sore evenings lighter.

The pungent mood of drying leaves rising,
Bob's banging rhythms are sounds of a free man,
A freight-train rider — a mean primer and curer
Of men.

**Another Man...**

Chill sunlight
Catches rusted corrugations,
Bent tin, rotting timbers,
That were home, resonant on Sunday
With John's guitar in a second room.
Porch collapsed last year in sunbleached pile,
Weathered remains are like bones from time long dead.
A vision of stones in old fields,
Sorrel and toadflax repossessing the pasture,
Greets her this dawn.
Already smoke billows from new brick chimneys,
Settles on brown sedge by the road.

Fall's frost found her unprepared for news of John:
Lost appeals and last-ditch failure, and
Today, deep South of here,
They will push a needle into his arm,
Pump poison 'til he's dead.
She inhales sweet gum, dusty like dried blood,
And thinks...

**Lawd, have mercy**
**Mercy on me...**

## A Bible Lesson

Jehovah, Chile, will strip you **down!**
Take yo' nose ring an' yo' tinklin' ornaments.
Knock off the biggity folks, too, Chile!
Who keep yo' face in the dus'.
So, Chile, don' be too proud to walk 'umble.
But, Honey,
Don' take no shit from white folks,
Neither.

**Flying Home**

The juke comes to silence.
Glasses motionless,
Even skittery girls listen,
And boasting men take seats.
Black Jake vamps his guitar once more,
Appreciates the quiet,
Then releases train rhythm
That rocks the low-ceiled roof,
Takes the freeze from bodies worked all week,
Creates a trembling web over chaos.
His words contrast the driving chords:
Are of muddy waters rising and lovers gone-by,
Best friends' treachery and hungry nights' journeying.
His French-harp whoop, guitar whoosh, voiced hollers refuse
    catastrophe the win!
Swooping, rushing, chugging up steep grades,
He pulls the juke along.
Knows success in the brightness of their eyes:
A syncopating community on high,
Rocking.

**Prodigal**

November rain liberates last gold,
Succulent copper,
Searing red of Carolina trees,
Beating earth in afternoon fury.
His cap dripping under deluge,
The son makes his way through unfurrowed fields,
Pushes aside branches,
Steps through ankle-deep underbrush. . . damp.

*(A single bird takes flight,*
*Describes slow circles above the clearing.)*

His gaze is fixed by ancestral stones,
Washed in autumn rain,
Guarded by spirits
Whose incantation and percussion have taught him
Blue-steel-and-train-whistle rites of southern life.
Kneeling, knees soaked in earth,
He touches his Father's mark,
Hums gratitude for ancient energies
Transfiguring earth.
He accosts the life above:

"You, Ole African! Reckon you ain't de only one's
Glad I'm home."

Rain.
A circling bird settles toward earth.
Liberated gold.
Succulent copper.
Searing red of Carolina fall.

## About the Author

Houston Baker was born in Louisville, Kentucky, a town called by some the "gateway" to the South, but designated by others a typical site on America's Dixie Pike. Louisville is Southern in its bourbon-laden air and its racialistic attitudes — attitudes that led to shotgun-toting, bus-burning opposition to egalitarian schooling a few years ago. During the author's youth the town was **dangerously** Southern for black ambitions and enterprises (like walking down the street). The effects of Louisville on Afro-America is a subject for a Myrdal study. The town's effects on the author, however, included a residue of hatred, bitterness, longing, and something else. . . That "something else" surfaced in North Carolina during a year's residence in 1982. Most miraculous memories arose like dawn fog over unharvested fields. The result was a dreadful love. Trees and sedges, birds and melodies, sleek pickups and beautiful black faces recalled Louisville and provided sure signs that the South is still the cradle of black personhood in these United States. North Carolina was a healing time; it carried me back to origins and thrust me forward to adult appreciations. My current collection of poems marks a distinctive place in my rambling (i.e., travelling, running) toward authentic blue/black Afro-American sound. The sound is one I thought I had missed during Louisville days. It was, however, undeniably there — to be found, or discovered, only after I agreed (willy-nilly) to confront the pain and unexpected pleasures of a blues journey home.

```
PS
3552      Baker, Houston A.
.A427         Blues journeys
B5        home:...
1985
```

**KNIGHT-CAPRON LIBRARY**
Lynchburg College
Lynchburg, Virginia   24501

APR 8 7

# STANDING TALL

*Standing Tall*

Copyright ©2002 by Quentin Road Ministries

All rights reserved

No part of this book may be reproduced or transmitted in any form or by any means, electronic or mechanical, including photocopying, recording, or by any information storage and retrieval system without permission in writing from Quentin Road Ministries, except in the case of brief quotations embodied in professional articles and reviews.

All Scripture quotations taken from the King James Version.

Quentin Road Ministries
60 Quentin Road
Lake Zurich, IL 60047

1-800-784-7223

ISBN: 0-9679145-5-8, thxjb